ROBERT TODD LINCOLN

MARY LINCOLN

THOMAS (TAD) LINCOLN

WHERE LINCOLN WALKED

RAYMOND BIAL

WALKER AND COMPANY

NEW YORK

—⬥—

First published in the United States of America in 1997 by Walker Publishing Company, Inc.

Published simultaneously in Canada by Thomas Allen & Son Canada, Limited, Markham, Ontario

Library of Congress Cataloging-in-Publication Data
Bial, Raymond
Where Lincoln Walked/Raymond Bial.
p. cm.
Includes bibliographical references and index.
Summary: Includes a brief biography of President Lincoln, a list of locations where he walked, and photographs of places, buildings, and objects significant in his life.
ISBN 0-8027-8630-8 (hardcover). —ISBN 0-8027-8631-6 (reinforced)
1. Lincoln, Abraham, 1809-1865—Juvenile literature. 2. Lincoln, Abraham, 1809-1865—Pictorial works—Juvenile literature. 3. Presidents—United States—Biography—Juvenile literature. 4. Presidents—United States—Pictorial works—Juvenile literature.
[1. Lincoln, Abraham, 1809-1865. 2. Presidents.] I. Title.
E457.905.B52 1997
973.7 ' 092—dc21

Historical photographs appearing on endpapers, title page, and pages 42, 43, and 45 are from the Illinois State Historical Library.

Maps on page 46 by Susan Carlson.

Book design by Snap-Haus Graphics

Printed in Hong Kong
10 9 8 7 6 5 4 3 2 1

ACKNOWLEDGMENTS

I am deeply grateful to the helpful and friendly staff at the following locations where the photographs for *Where Lincoln Walked* were made: Lincoln Homestead State Park (near Springfield, Kentucky), Abraham Lincoln Birthplace (Sinking Spring Farm), Abraham Lincoln's Boyhood Home (Knob Creek Farm), Lincoln Boyhood National Memorial (Pigeon Creek, Indiana), Lincoln's New Salem, Vandalia Statehouse, Postville Courthouse, Lincoln Home National Historic Site, the Old State Capitol, Lincoln-Herndon Law Offices, and the Springfield Illinois Convention and Visitors Bureau.

I would also like to thank Mary Michals and Kim Bauer of the Illinois State Historical Society for their assistance with information and illustrations, and my editor, Emily Easton, for believing in this book. As always, I would like to offer deepest thanks to my wife, Linda, and my children—Anna, Sarah, and Luke—for their wonderful support.

On a cold February morning in 1809, Nancy Hanks Lincoln settled on a bed of bear skins and corn husks in a small cabin and gave birth to a son. The baby was named Abraham, after his grandfather, and was called Abe for short. "It is a great folly to attempt to make anything out of me or my early life," Abraham Lincoln later said of his childhood, referring to those years as "the short and simple annals of the poor." Yet the events of young Abe's rugged youth in the woods and prairie shaped him into a remarkable man, who would become a great president.

Before she married Thomas Lincoln, Nancy Hanks made her home in a cabin near Springfield, Kentucky. She slept upstairs, likely never imagining that she would someday become mother to the president.

Nancy Hanks spent her days mending clothes and cooking with iron pots over an open fire in a hearth no different from the one in the cabin where she lived and worked before she married Thomas Lincoln in 1806.

Kentucky was still a wilderness filled with danger and hardship when the Lincolns settled there. Abe's grandfather had been killed by an Indian while working in the fields with his eight-year-old son Thomas in May 1786. Great events are often influenced by small acts; if Thomas had not been saved by his older brother that day, his son Abe would never have been born. Abe later described his father as "a wandering laboring boy" who "grew up literally without education." Thomas married Nancy Hanks on June 10, 1806. He worked a number of odd jobs, mostly as a carpenter, and hunted with his musket in the woods to put wild game on the family table. On pleasant afternoons Nancy sometimes left the dark cabin and walked the hillsides with their baby, Abraham, in her arms.

Sinking Spring Farm was named after a deep spring that trickled over the moss-covered rocks in a cavern on a hillside. Nearby, in a one-room cabin with just one door and one window, Abe Lincoln was born on February 12, 1809.

Abraham spent his early years in this one-room cabin with red clay chinking near Hodgenville, Kentucky. Having moved here when he was two years old, Abe said, "My earliest recollection is of the Knob Creek place."

When Abe was two years old, the Lincoln family decided to move from the limestone hills of Sinking Spring to the red clay fields at Knob Creek. Like other frontier children, Abe grew up carrying water, bringing in wood for the fireplace, working in the fields, and getting his education "by littles." Occasionally, he and his older sister, Sarah, walked two miles to a log school with a dirt floor. Since there were no books at this "blab school," they recited their lessons out loud.

Once, while playing on a log in Knob Creek, Abe fell in and would have drowned in the flooded stream if his boyhood friend Austin Gollaher had not fished him out with a sycamore branch.

The Lincoln family settled in the deep woods of Pigeon Creek, Indiana, in December 1816 and set to work carving a homestead out of the wilderness, where panthers screamed in the night, and wolves howled far off in the distance.

In December 1816, the Lincoln family moved north to Indiana. Abe was just seven years old as they ferried across the shimmering Ohio River and made their way deep into the woods to Pigeon Creek. "It was a wild region, with many bears and other wild animals still in the woods," he later recalled. Thomas first put up a half-camp, a crude lean-to made of sticks and logs, to shelter his family from the cold and wind. Until spring the family lived almost entirely on wild game—squirrels, rabbits, turkeys, geese, and an occasional bear. Abe later remembered that first winter as one of the bleakest times in his life; smoke blew into the half-camp, rain and snow dripped from the roof, and the log walls barely cut the wind. In February, when Abe turned eight, his father built a one-room log cabin that was eighteen feet square with a hard-packed dirt floor, a log chimney lined with clay, and a stone fireplace.

"Here I grew up," Abe said, describing his life in this one-room cabin in Indiana as "pretty pinching times."

The following year tragedy struck the Lincoln family—the first of many sad events that would darken Abe's life—when an epidemic of the "milk sick" swept through the Indiana frontier. It was later discovered that the illness is caused by drinking the milk of cows that have eaten white snakeroot, a deadly plant that grows in deep shade. But at the time, the cause of milk sickness was a mystery. Nancy, who had been caring for sick relatives, fell ill and died on October 5, 1818, at the age of thirty-five. "Be good and kind to your father," she told Abe and Sarah on her deathbed, "and to one another and the world." Brokenhearted, Abe helped his father by making pegs and planing boards for his mother's coffin.

People on the frontier often drank milk, especially when they were ill, to maintain their strength. Little did they know that the nourishing drink might contain a deadly poison.

In late 1819, Thomas Lincoln traveled to Elizabethtown, Kentucky, and married Sarah Bush Johnston, a widow with three children, whom he had known since he was a young man. When she arrived at the Pigeon Creek cabin, Sarah commented that the Lincoln children had to be dressed to look "more human." By all accounts, she loved Abe and his sister, and was a strong, positive influence in their lives. About Abe, she said frankly, "He was the best boy I ever saw."

Eight people lived in the little cabin, where Sarah Lincoln cooked at the hearth and served meals to the Lincoln family at a puncheon table and benches. Climbing up pegs driven into the walls, Abe slept in the loft.

It is believed that Abe didn't get along very well with his father. Some people said Thomas beat Abe for reading too many books and generally wishing to be educated; others contended that Abe was hostile toward his father. However, his stepmother, Sarah, proved to be a steady force in his life, guiding him to learn as much as possible and make something of his life. Over Thomas's objections, she also sent Abe to the local school. The young man became the best speller in the school, and at home he did all the writing for his family. His sense of humor was already evident in a poem he wrote:

> Abraham Lincoln
> his hand and pen
> he will be good but
> god knows when

Azy Dorsey, one of his teachers, recalled that Abe walked to the log schoolhouse in a raccoon cap, moccasins, and buckskin clothes made from tanned deer hide.

He ciphered, or solved math problems, on a wooden board, then shaved the numbers off with a knife for the next lesson. He read many books, such as *The Life of Washington, Aesop's Fables, Robinson Crusoe,* and *Pilgrim's Progress.* After reading *The Arabian Nights,* his cousin Dennis Hanks claimed the book was filled with lies. "Mighty darn good lies," Abe replied. In total, Abe had less than a year's formal education, but he loved to read and tell stories. His love of books was legendary; he reportedly read every book to be found within fifty miles of his home in the Indiana woods.

When plowing fields in the spring, Abe was sometimes caught reading a book at the end of a furrow while allowing the horse to "breathe," or rest. "My father taught me to work," he once said, "but he didn't teach me to like it."

When he was seventeen, Abe left home and went to work for thirty-seven cents a day, doing "the roughest work a young man could be made to do." He built a small scow, or flat-bottomed boat, and ferried travelers across the wide Ohio River. Then, just a year and a half after she was married, his sister, Sarah, died in childbirth. Nineteen-year-old Abe was devastated, having lost first his mother and now his beloved sister. In his grief, he worked harder than ever, and that spring, perhaps to get away from the sorrows of his Indiana home, he agreed to take a flat-boat of farm produce to New Orleans for James Gentry. It was the first city Abe had ever seen, and the young man who had spent his entire life in the wilderness was fascinated. Of all the sights, it was the slave market that made an enduring impression on him. Gentry's son recalled,

Tall and strong for his age, Abe "had an ax put into his hands at once." For the next fifteen years he was "constantly handling that most useful instrument" as he battled "with the trees and logs and grubs."

"We stood and watched slaves sold and Abe was very angry." Having sold their flatboat, the two men booked passage on a steamboat back to Indiana. As was the custom during those times, Abe dutifully gave his father the twenty-four dollars he had earned for the three-month trip.

The Lincoln family attended the Pigeon Creek Baptist Church, a log cabin built by Thomas Lincoln. Abe also hung around Gentryville, the local trading post, where he listened to stories and swapped a few yarns of his own with local folks and travelers. He began to visit the log courthouse, where he observed lawyers arguing cases. Fascinated by the law, he read a borrowed set of the *Revised Statutes of Indiana* and studied the Declaration of Independence as well as the U. S. Constitution, then watched intently as lawyers debated the documents in the courtroom.

Abe first studied law books in Indiana, where he lived from the age of seven until he was twenty-one. Years later, he became a lawyer in Illinois by reading books late into the night.

In February 1830, having heard of the fertile prairies of Illinois, Thomas sold the Pigeon Creek farm, and the family, including twenty-one-year-old Abe, moved there. Abe returned to Pigeon Creek just once more in his life, in 1844. The trip to this place where his mother was buried evoked such strong feelings in him that he later wrote poetry about it. The Lincolns forded the Wabash River at Vincennes, Indiana, and traveled the rough frontier for two weeks until they arrived at a site near Decatur, Illinois. They built a cabin in a clearing among the oak trees, and that summer Abe and his stepbrother John Hanks split thousands of fence rails for neighboring farmers—rails that decades later earned him the nickname of "the Rail-splitter."

Thomas Lincoln partly wanted to move to Illinois to get away from the milk sickness. Abe's mother, Nancy Hanks, was buried in the shady woods near the Lincoln farm on Pigeon Creek.

Most of the family fell ill that autumn with chills and fever—a sickness called ague. Then the winter of 1830–31 set in with a blizzard that was followed by sheets of freezing rain and more "big snows." The temperature plunged to twelve degrees below zero for many days. Livestock died in the fields, and many settlers froze to death. Thomas became so discouraged that he decided to return to Indiana. That spring, he and Sarah, along with most of the family, headed back but ended up settling instead near Lerna, Illinois, where they lived for the rest of their lives.

Abe was a very strong young man. A neighbor once said, "If you heard him felling trees in a clearing, you would think there were three men at work, the way the trees fell." Abe then split the logs into rails for fences.

Separating from his family, this time for good, Abe and John Hanks hired on with Denton Offutt to guide another flatboat to New Orleans. In mid-April, the two young men set off with Offutt down the Sangamon River on a flatboat loaded with barreled pork, live hogs, and corn. They had traveled only a few miles downriver when the flatboat got hung up briefly on a dam near New Salem. Offutt was impressed with the village of New Salem, and when they returned from New Orleans he opened a store there and hired Abe, who already considered himself "a piece of floating driftwood," to be a clerk. His friendly "Howdy," lively yarns, and reputation for honesty soon made Abe a well-liked young man in the village. It is said he once walked six miles to give back a few cents he had overcharged a woman for dry goods.

At its height in 1833, New Salem had twenty-five families and a number of

Headed for the bustling city of New Orleans, Abe floated down the Sangamon River, but on the way his flatboat got hung up on a dam near the village of New Salem.

businesses: tavern, blacksmith, cooper, wheelwright, tanner, and several dry goods stores, as well as a log schoolhouse. At the time, Chicago was just a cluster of cabins around Fort Dearborn, and most of Illinois was still frontier. Hardy families provided for themselves, but there were also dances, cabin raisings, and quilting bees, as well as political rallies. Folks enjoyed barbecues on the Fourth of July that included plenty of long speeches and intense, sweaty contests. Becoming part of the community, Abe demonstrated his strength by wrestling one of the boys who lived in nearby Clary Grove to a draw, and his intelligence by joining the debating society. Then, in 1832, he ran as a Whig Party candidate for the Illinois legislature. He lost the election, but a small fire was kindled within him—an interest in attaining political office through which he might help others.

The dam on which Abe's flatboat got stuck was located just below this grist- and sawmill. Powered by a waterwheel, the mill was built by John M. Camron in 1828 when he purchased the land on which New Salem was laid out.

In 1832, Abe became partners with William Berry in this store, known today as the "First Berry-Lincoln Store." When a larger frame building became available just down the road, the partners moved there in January 1833.

During the campaign, Offutt's store failed and Abe lost his job. He became a partner with William Berry in another store, which occupied two locations in New Salem, and then postmaster from 1833 to 1836. He eagerly read the newspapers that arrived in the village and was known to keep the mail in his tall hat as he walked around New Salem making his deliveries.

The "Second Berry-Lincoln Store" not only sold dry goods but also was a place where folks gathered to swap stories, discuss the weather, and argue the politics of the day. Abe often stood behind this counter, passing the time of day with customers.

Abe often boarded at this tavern built and operated by James Rutledge, who cofounded New Salem with John Camron. By law, tavern rates were fixed at thirty-seven and a half cents per day for a meal and overnight stay.

As when he was a boy, Abe climbed a wooden ladder and slept in the loft of the Rutledge Tavern. When he came to New Salem, he was a rough, awkward young man, but through hard work and study, he left as a skillful lawyer and respected leader.

Never having a home of his own in New Salem, he boarded with other families, sleeping in the lofts of their cabins and at the Rutledge Tavern, where he met and fell in love with Ann Rutledge, daughter of the innkeeper. Elected to the state legislature in 1834, he was probably looking forward to a bright future with Ann when the lovely young woman came down with a fever and died suddenly at the age of twenty-two. Much has been made of Abe's affection for her, some saying she was the great love of his life. Abe was left more melancholy than ever; his friend and law partner William H. Herndon later wrote that "the snows and rain that fell upon her grave filled him with indescribable grief."

Abe took his meals seated around a table with the family and other boarders at the Rutledge Tavern. Here, he met and fell deeply in love with Ann Rutledge.

When Abe was elected to the Illinois legislature, he became a vigorous representative of the people in these chambers at the old state capitol in Vandalia. He served as a state representative here from 1834 to 1839.

Despite undergoing yet another tragic episode in his life, Abe forged ahead with his career. Borrowing two hundred dollars, he bought a new suit, paid off a couple of debts, and took the stagecoach to the state capital in Vandalia for the busy legislative session. There he met Stephen A. Douglas of Jacksonville, who would later become his political adversary. Short-statured Douglas was nicknamed "the Little Giant," and Abe, who stood six feet four inches tall, described him as "the least man he had ever seen." During the session, the legislature discussed bridges, roads, and ferries, but also difficult issues such as slavery, with Abe helping to ensure that Illinois would remain a free state. He was reelected twice and became the floor leader of the Whig Party.

In the Illinois State Supreme Court chambers at the state capitol in Vandalia, Abe was admitted to the bar, meaning he could practice law. As a young lawyer, he also argued cases before the judges in this courtroom.

25

Meanwhile, Abe read law books on his own and was licensed as an attorney on September 9, 1836. At that time, licenses were mostly certificates of good character—and Abe was certainly a man of the best character. He moved to Springfield, which became the state capital in 1839, and lived in lodgings above Joshua Speed's General Store. When Abe arrived, Speed gazed at him and thought, "I never saw so gloomy and melancholy a face in my life." Abe took his saddlebags up to his room, returned downstairs, and reported, "Well, Speed, I'm moved."

Abe worked for three years in a law firm with John Todd Stuart, then entered into a law partnership with Stephen T. Logan for another three years, after which he became partners with William H. Herndon. For the next twenty-one years—even while Abe was president—the two men remained partners and best friends.

Among the many places where Abe traveled on the circuit was the Postville Courthouse, often loping along on horseback or driving his own buggy, "a homemade affair, drawn by a horse of scant qualities."

While Herndon stayed home and looked after the office, Abe began riding the Eighth Circuit in 1839. Because of the sparse population of most counties in the state, a system was created in which a judge and lawyers traveled from county to county on a circuit to hear cases. It was a rough life, but Abe loved crossing the broad, windswept prairie, and swapping stories with lawyers and local folks. Every spring and autumn for more than a dozen years, he followed Judge David Davis around central Illinois on what amounted to a four-hundred-mile journey through Beardstown, Metamora, Mount Pulaski, Postville, Urbana, and other county seats. During his travels, Abe became well known for his humor in the courtroom.

Abe argued many cases before a jury seated in these chairs at the Postville Courthouse. It was a rough life, with lawyers often meeting with clients under shade trees, but Abe enjoyed traveling the countryside and meeting people along the way.

While he was practicing law, Abe met Mary Ann Todd. From a well-to-do Kentucky family, she was just five foot two, bright, and pretty, with a turned-up nose that Abe liked. They met at a ball, where he came up to her and said, "Miss Todd, I would like to dance with you in the worst way." Mary later said that he was so awkward on his feet that he did indeed dance with her "in the worst way." Abe began courting her, and toward the end of 1840 they were engaged. Although Mary's parents disapproved of Abe, they agreed upon a wedding in their home. That week, Abe wrote to a lawyer in Shawneetown, "Nothing new here, except for my marrying, which to me, is a matter of profound wonder."

In 1842, two years after their marriage, the Lincolns moved into this two-story clapboard house at the corner of Eighth and Jackson Streets. Located near downtown Springfield, it was just a leisurely stroll for Abe to the state capitol and his law office.

Their first child, Robert Todd Lincoln, was born on August 1, 1843, and two years later the Lincolns were blessed with another son, whom they named Eddie. During this time, Abe was earning a very good income of about fifteen hundred dollars a year, and in January 1847, he purchased a frame house on the corner of Eighth and Jackson Streets—the only home he would ever own in his life. By all accounts, the Lincolns had a loving, happy marriage at this time. Mary occasionally displayed a sharp tongue and hot temper, and Abe would retreat to his law offices down the street. Yet he was caring when she had one of her frequent migraine headaches, and she encouraged him in his career.

Abe often sat at this desk in the corner of his bedroom on the second floor of his Springfield home. Here, he composed speeches and letters until the day he left for Washington, D.C., as the newly elected president.

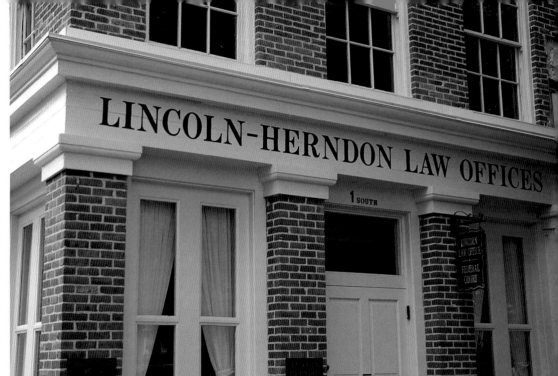

When Abe ran for the Illinois Seventh Congressional District seat, in 1846, he was given two hundred dollars by the Whig Party for the campaign but easily defeated Democrat Peter Cartright, a fire-and-brimstone evangelist. He returned all the money except for the seventy-five cents he had spent on a barrel of cider for some farmers at a political rally. He leased his Springfield house, and the Lincolns moved to Washington, D.C., a large city of forty thousand people that was the center of both the federal government and the slave trade, with gangs of slaves in chains routinely passing by the Capitol Building. The Lincolns were not happy living in Washington with its dirty streets, gambling houses, and saloons; Mary stayed just three months, then took their sons and went to live with her family in Lexington, Kentucky.

When Abe wasn't riding the circuit, he shared this Springfield office with Billy Herndon. The office was located at Sixth and Adams Streets on the second floor of a brick building, which for a time also housed the federal court in Illinois.

Disappointed with politics, Abe returned to Springfield in 1849 to practice law with Billy Herndon. The two men rented space in various locations in Springfield, their messy offices tending to overflow with stacks of papers. The partners were just as disorganized in their record keeping. Abe kept an envelope on which he'd written, "If you can't find it anywhere else, look in here." Abe kept their money equally divided in two envelopes: one with his name and the other marked "Herndon's half." He once said, "Billy and I never had the scratch of a pen between us . . . we just divide as we go along."

The tables in the Lincoln-Herndon law office were arranged in a T shape when Abe and Billy met clients. From their office windows, they had an excellent view of the state capitol, which was just across the street.

Tragedy struck the Lincoln household on February 1, 1850, when four-year-old Eddie died, possibly of diptheria. In grief, Abe immersed himself in his work, and Mary took comfort in religion. Mary became pregnant and had another child, William Wallace, in December 1850, who helped to brighten their home again. However, Abe's father lay dying in late 1851. Despite repeated letters from his stepbrother, Abe never visited him, perhaps because he was still angry with him. He only sent a final message "to remember to call upon, and confide in, our great, and good, and merciful Maker." When Thomas died, Abe, who had not seen his father in ten years, did not attend the funeral. The Lincolns' fourth child was born in April 1853, and he was named Thomas after his grandfather. Because he had a large head and wriggled like a tadpole, he was nicknamed "Tad."

When he came home from his law office or the circuit, Abe enjoyed playing with his boys on the parlor floor. He lay on the carpet in the warmth of the hearth and tossed the young ones into the air.

The Lincoln boys played with their wooden toys and slept in a comfortable bed in this room in their Springfield home. However, a dark shadow was cast over the family when young Eddie died.

33

Abe had given up politics, but the pro-slavery activities of his old rival Stephen A. Douglas drew Abe to the state Republican convention in Bloomington in 1856. Abe helped to draft a platform and a slate of candidates for the party in Illinois. Asked to give a brief, impromptu speech, he spoke for one and a half hours so eloquently that the crowd was mesmerized. Even reporters were so spellbound that they didn't take notes and no record was ever made of what became known as the "Lost Speech."

At the state capitol, Abe argued more than two hundred cases before the state supreme court, served in the legislature, studied at the law library, and made many speeches. He was a daily visitor until he left Springfield to become president.

On June 16, 1858, Illinois Republicans nominated Abe to run against Stephen A. Douglas for the Senate seat "the Little Giant" had held for over ten years. Abe accepted with his famous "House Divided" speech in the state capitol building, in which he declared: "A house divided against itself cannot stand. I believe this Government cannot endure, permanently half slave and half free. I do not expect the Union to be dissolved—I do not expect the house to fall—but I do expect it will cease to be divided. It will become all one thing, or all the other."

While serving in the legislature, Abe sat in the Illinois Hall of Representatives. When he ran for the United States Senate against Stephen A. Douglas, he made his "House Divided" speech from this podium.

One of the Lincoln-Douglas debates was held at Old Main on the campus of Knox College in Galesburg. Lincoln and Douglas stood at the side doors of the building to address the thousands of people who had gathered before them.

Through the late summer and early autumn, the two men engaged in what became the most important and famous debates in U.S. history. Beginning in August, they met at Ottawa, Freeport, Jonesboro, Charleston, Galesburg, Quincy, and Alton. At Clinton, Lincoln followed a three-hour speech by Douglas with his famous advice, "You can fool all of the people part of the time and part of the people all of the time, but you cannot fool all of the people all of the time." The two contrasted not only in appearance—Lincoln tall and lean, Douglas short and squat—but also in character: Abe was a man of principles, whereas Douglas was a bigot and a crafty politician. Douglas admitted that Abe would be difficult to defeat because he "is as honest as he is shrewd." Douglas dressed elegantly and traveled in style, while Abe wore rumpled clothing and rode on ordinary trains.

During the Galesburg debate in western Illinois, Abe said eloquently that Stephen Douglas "is blowing out the moral lights around us when he contends that whoever wants slaves has a right to hold them."

Although Abraham Lincoln lost the race for United States senator, many Americans were so impressed by his ideas that he was nominated to run for president—a campaign against Stephen A. Douglas that he easily won.

At that time, senators were selected by their state legislatures, and Lincoln lost the election when Democrats outnumbered Republicans in the Illinois legislature. "I feel just like the little boy who stubbed his toe," he said afterward. "I am too big to cry and too badly hurt to laugh." However, during the campaign, Abe received considerable national attention for his intelligence and ability. Two years later he was nominated as the Republican candidate for president of the United States. His supporters portrayed him as "Honest Abe" and "the Rail-splitter." Once again his Democratic opponent was Stephen A. Douglas, but this time Abe easily defeated the little man from Jacksonville.

Every morning, square-jawed Abe shaved off his whiskers with a sharp razor. However, when he became president, a girl wrote to Abe and convinced him that he would appear more dignified if he grew a beard.

After he left home, Abe seldom visited this two-room
cabin of Thomas and Sarah Lincoln near Goosenest
Prairie. However, on his way to Washington, he visited his stepmother at a nearby home to say good-bye.

Abe accepted the presidency reluctantly. After his election, the nation was torn apart, with six states seceding from the Union before he took the oath of office. The task before him was as great as that which had faced the founding fathers—to save a nation. On his last day in Springfield, he visited Billy Herndon. Noticing the Lincoln and Herndon sign swinging in the breeze, Abe said, "Let it hang there undisturbed. Give our clients to understand that the election of a President makes no change in the firm of Lincoln and Herndon. If I live I'm coming back some time, and we'll go right on practicing law as if nothing ever happened." On his way to Washington, Abe stopped to visit his family on January 30, 1861, and Sarah Lincoln had a sense of foreboding that she would never see Abe again.

Abe enjoyed practicing law and he hoped to someday come home to friends and family, but he also had a sad sense of foreboding. When he left Springfield, he said, "I now leave, not knowing when, or whether ever, I may return."

If the republic were to be saved, it would take a man of extraordinary strength and intelligence. Having lost those dearest to him (mother, sister, Ann Rutledge, and then his own child), Abe knew how to prevail over tragedy. He skillfully led the nation through the Civil War—the most horrible war in U.S. history, during which a million people were killed or wounded—only to be murdered by John Wilkes Booth early in his second term. General Robert E. Lee, who had surrendered his army as much to Lincoln's compassion as to Ulysses S. Grant's unrelenting attacks, was shocked. He had trusted that Lincoln would treat the defeated southern states fairly while building a "just and lasting peace." As the president had stated, he intended to treat everyone "with malice toward none; with charity for all; with firmness in the right,

In his second inaugural address, dated March 4, 1865, Abe spoke eloquently of the need "to bind up the nation's wounds" after the terrible suffering of the Civil War. Barely a month later, he was murdered by John Wilkes Booth.

INAUGURAL ADDRESS

OF

ABRAHAM LINCOLN

MARCH 4th, 1865.

Fellow-Countrymen:

At this second appearing to take the oath of the Presidential office there is less occasion for an extended address than there was at the first. Then a statement, somewhat in detail of a course to be pursued, seemed fitting and proper. Now, at the expiration of four years, during which public declarations have been constantly called forth on every point and phase of the great contest which still absorbs the attention and engrosses the energies of the nation, little that is new could be presented. The progress of our arms upon which all else chiefly depends, is as well known to the public as to myself: and it is, I trust, reasonably satisfactory and encouraging to all. With high hope for the future, no prediction in regard to it is ventured.

On the occasion corresponding to it four years ago, all thoughts were anxiously directed to an impending civil war. All dreaded it—all sought to avert it. When the inaugural address was being delivered from this place, devoted altogether to saving the Union without war, insurgent agents were in the city seeking to destroy it without war—seeking to dissolve the Union and divide the effects by negotiation. Both parties deprecated war:

BUT ONE OF THEM WOULD *MAKE* WAR RATHER THAN LET THE NATION SURVIVE; AND THE OTHER WOULD *ACCEPT* WAR RATHER THAN LET IT PERISH. AND THE WAR CAME.

One eighth of the whole population were colored slaves, not distributed generally over the Union, but localized in the southern part of it. These slaves constituted a peculiar and powerful interest. All knew that this interest was somehow, the cause of the war. To strengthen, perpetuate, and extend this interest was the object for which the insurgents would rend the Union, even by war; while the Government claimed no right to do more than to restrict the territorial enlargement of it. Neither party expected for the war the magnitude or the duration which it has already attained. Neither anticipated that the cause of the conflict might cease with, or even before, the conflict itself should cease. Each looked for an easier triumph, and a result less fundamental and astounding. Both read the same Bible, and pray to the same God; and each invokes His aid against the other. It may seem strange that any man should dare to ask a just God's assistance in wringing their bread from the sweat of other men's faces; but let us judge not, that we be not judged. The prayers of both could not be answered; that of neither has been answered fully. The Almighty has His own purpose.

"WOE UNTO THE WORLD BECAUSE OF OFFENCES! FOR IT MUST NEEDS BE THAT OFFENCES COME; BUT WOE TO THAT MAN BY WHOM THE OFFENCE COMETH."

If we shall suppose that American slavery is one of those offences which, in the providence of God, must needs come, but which, having continued through his appointed time, he now wills to remove, and that he gives to both North and South this terrible war, as the woe due to those by whom the offence came, shall we discern therein any departure from those divine attributes which the believers in a living God always ascribe to him?

Fondly do we hope—fervently do we pray—that this mighty scourge of war may soon pass away. Yet, if God wills that it continue until all the wealth piled by the bondman's two hundred and fifty years of unrequited toil shall be sunk, and until every drop of blood drawn with the lash shall be paid with another drawn with the sword, as was said three thousand years ago, so still it must be said,

"THE JUDGMENTS OF THE LORD ARE TRUE AND RIGHTEOUS ALTOGETHER."

WITH MALICE TOWARDS NONE; WITH CHARITY FOR ALL; WITH FIRMNESS IN THE RIGHT, AS GOD GIVES US TO SEE THE RIGHT, LET US STRIVE ON TO FINISH THE WORK WE ARE IN; TO BIND UP THE NATION'S WOUNDS; TO CARE FOR HIM WHO SHALL HAVE BORNE THE BATTLE, AND FOR HIS WIDOW AND HIS ORPHAN; TO DO ALL WHICH MAY ACHIEVE AND CHERISH A JUST AND A LASTING PEACE AMONG OURSELVES, AND WITH ALL NATIONS.

Jas. B. Rodgers, Printer. 52 & 54 North Sixth St., Phil.

as God gives us to see the right, let us strive on to finish the work we are in; to bind up the nation's wounds; to care for him who shall have borne the battle, and for his widow and his orphan—to do all which may achieve and cherish a just and lasting peace among ourselves, and with all nations."

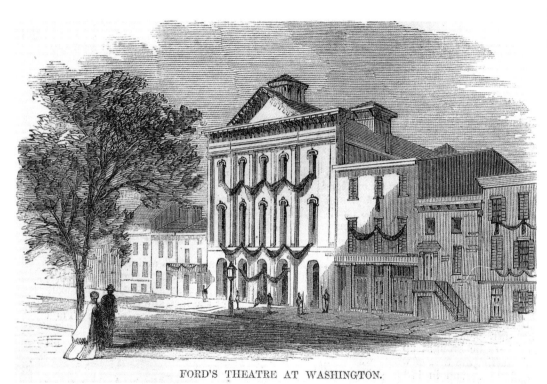

FORD'S THEATRE AT WASHINGTON.

The play Our American Cousin *was playing to a full house at Ford's Theatre, where the Lincolns were seated in the upper-right-hand box, when Abe was shot on April 14, 1865. Carried to a home across the street, Abe died there at 7:22 A.M. the next morning.*

Upon Abe's death, Secretary of War Edwin Stanton said, "Now he belongs to the Ages." Abe's body lay in state in the Capitol while over seventy-five thousand people paid their respects. Crowds gathered all along the rambling 1,662-mile journey to Baltimore, Harrisburg, Philadelphia, New York, Albany, Buffalo, Cleveland, Columbus, Indianapolis, Chicago, and finally Springfield. Abe came home to Springfield not to live in his old home and practice law with Billy Herndon, but to be buried.

As a carefree young man, Abe wore a straw hat; as an older man with solemn responsibilities, he wore the tall felt hat that became his trademark.

Upon the death of her stepson, Sarah Lincoln said, "I did not want Abe to run for President and I did not want to see him elected. . . . When he came down to see me, after he was elected President . . . my heart told me . . . that I should never see him again." But Abraham Lincoln knew his duty, and, as his father had taught him, he knew how to work, even if he didn't always like it. Though he died that dark evening at Ford's Theatre, the light of his words and the example of his life continue to shine brightly for the United States and the world.

After he was elected president, a dignified Abraham Lincoln sat for this portrait which was taken by Alexander Gardner at the Mathew Brady Studio in Washington, D. C., on February 24, 1861.

PLACES TO VISIT

Among the many fascinating places where Abraham Lincoln walked on the "Lincoln Heritage Trail" are the following state and national sites. Many of the photographs for this book were made at these locations, and they are definitely worth visiting on family vacations or weekend trips. Those wishing to visit any of these places may write or call the sites for additional information.

Lincoln Homestead State Park
Lincoln Park Road
Springfield, KY 40069
606-336-7461

Lincoln Birthplace National Historic Site
2995 Lincoln Farm Road
Hodgenville, KY 42748
502-358-3874

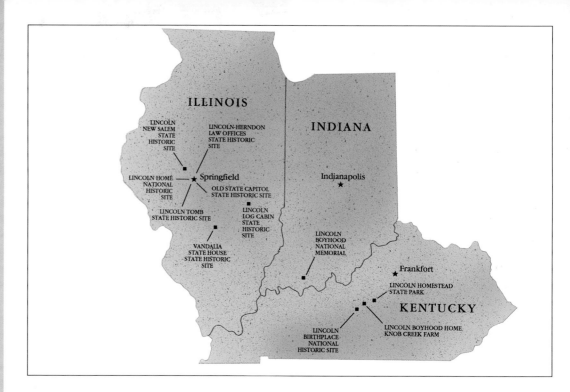

Knob Creek Farm
U.S. 31E
Hodgenville, KY 42748
502-549-3741

Lincoln Boyhood National Memorial
Lincoln City, IN 47552
812-937-4541

Lincoln's New Salem State Historic Site
R. R. 1, P. O. Box 244A
Petersburg, IL 62675
217-632-7953

Vandalia Statehouse State Historic Site
315 West Gallatin
Vandalia, IL 62471
618-283-1161

Springfield Convention and Visitors Bureau
(for information about Lincoln-Herndon Law Offices, the Old State Capitol, Lincoln Depot Museum, and Lincoln's Tomb State Historic Site)
109 North Seventh Street
Springfield, IL 62701
800-545-7300

Old State Capitol State Historic Site
Springfield, IL 62701
217-785-7960

Lincoln-Herndon Law Offices State Historic Site
209 South Sixth Street
Springfield, IL 62701
217-785-7289

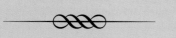

Lincoln Home National Historic Site
426 South Seventh Street
Springfield, IL 62701
217-789-2357

Postville Courthouse State Historic Site
P. O. Box 355
Lincoln, IL 62656
217-732-8930

Mt. Pulaski Courthouse State Historic Site
City Square
Mt. Pulaski, IL 62548
217-792-3919

Metamora Courthouse State Historic Site
113 East Partridge
Metamora, IL 61548
309-367-4470

Beardstown Courthouse
Beardstown Chamber of Commerce
212-B Washington Street
Beardstown, IL 62618
217-323-3271

Bryant Cottage State Historic Site
146 East Wilson Street
Bement, IL 61813
217-678-8184

Knox College
Galesburg Area Chamber of Commerce
154 East Simmons Street
Galesburg, IL 61401
309-343-1194

Lincoln Log Cabin State Historic Site
R.R.1, P. O. Box 175
Lerna, IL 62440
217-345-6489

FURTHER READING

Over the years, many excellent books have been written about Abraham Lincoln. Among them, the following were consulted in writing *Where Lincoln Walked*. *In Lincoln's Footsteps* and *Lincoln Parks* are especially useful if one would like to visit important historical sites. Of all the biographies of Abraham Lincoln, I believe Sandburg's two-volume set best captures the spirit of the man.

Burlingame, Michael. *The Inner World of Abraham Lincoln*. Urbana, Ill.: University of Illinois Press, 1994.

An Oral History of Abraham Lincoln: John G. Nicolay's Interview and Essays. Carbondale, Ill.: Southern Illinois University Press, 1996.

Davenport, Don. *In Lincoln's Footsteps: A Historical Guide to the Lincoln Sites in Illinois, Indiana, and Kentucky*. Madison, Wis.: Prairie Oak Press, 1991.

Fehrenbacher, Don E. *Prelude to Greatness: Lincoln in the 1850s*. Stanford, Calif.: Stanford University Press, 1962.

Hanchett, William. *Out of the Wilderness: The Life of Abraham Lincoln*. Urbana, Ill.: University of Illinois Press, 1994.

Holzer, Harold. *Dear Mr. Lincoln: Letters to the President*. Reading, Mass.: Addison-Wesley, 1993.

Lincoln, Abraham. *Speeches and Writings: 1859–1865*. New York: Library of America, 1989

McPherson, James M. *"We Cannot Escape History": Lincoln and the Last Best Hope of Earth*. Urbana, Ill.: University of Illinois Press, 1995.

Simon, Paul. *Lincoln's Preparation for Greatness: The Illinois Legislative Years*. Urbana, Ill.: University of Illinois Press, 1971.

Thomas, Benjamin P. *Lincoln's New Salem*. Carbondale, Ill.: Southern Illinois University Press, 1981.

Waldron, Larry. *Lincoln Parks: The Story Behind the Scenery*. Las Vegas, Nev.: KC Publications, 1986.

Zall, P. M., ed. *Abe Lincoln Laughing*. Berkeley, Calif.: University of California Press, 1982.

Young readers may be especially interested in the following books, some of which were also consulted in the research for *Where Lincoln Walked:*

Freedman, Russell. *Lincoln: A Photobiography*. New York: Clarion Books, 1987.

Lincoln, Abraham. *The Gettysburg Address*. Illustrated by Michael McCurdy. Boston: Houghton Mifflin, 1995.

Lincoln in His Own Words. Edited by Milton Meltzer. San Diego: Harcourt Brace, 1993.

Sandburg, Carl. *Abe Lincoln Grows Up*. New York: Harcourt Brace and World, 1926.

Sandburg, Carl. *Abraham Lincoln: The Prairie Years*. New York: Harcourt Brace and World, 1926.

INDEX

WILLIAM (WILLIE) LINCOLN

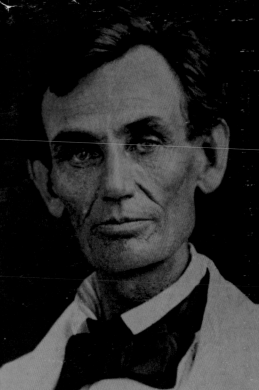

ABRAHAM LINCOLN, 1858

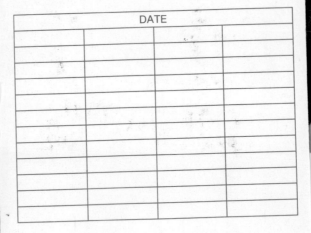

jB
LINCOLN   Bial, Raymond.
               Where Lincoln
               walked.

$17.85

DATE